Praise for
Illuminate: Harnessing the Positive Power of Negative Thinking

"Dave Corbin is the Illuminator! He is the ultimate authority to teach the positive power of negative thinking. He reaches inside you and lights up your soul. Illuminate is more than a book. It's a secret code to breakthrough thinking and powerful living. Read it, and watch your life illuminate right before your very eyes."

—Mitch Axelrod is the CEO (Chief Encouragement Officer™) of "The NEW Game™", author of *The NEW Game of Business*™!

"Illuminate: Harnessing the Positive Power of Negative Thinking is the winning combination of a thoroughly engaging story wrapped around a profoundly powerful management idea. Even before I'd finished reading it, I found myself thinking about how I can apply the Find It, Follow It, Fix It formula in my own work and life. David Corbin is a real-life Calvin Deere – wise, insightful, irreverent, and totally relevant. As he shows, accentuating the positive and illuminating the negative are the yin and yang of a managing a successful business, fostering positive relationships at work and at home, and making values more than just good intentions."

—Joe Tye, CEO of Values Coach Inc. and creator of *The Twelve Core Action Values*

"Illuminate will charge you with energy, and fill you with commitment. You will tap your creative genius like never before. If you are ready for breakthrough results and sustainable improvement, Illuminate. Make sure you and everyone in your organization reads this book.

—Larry Wilson, founder, Wilson Learning Systems, Pecos River Ranch, and author of *Playing to Win*

"I was immediately drawn to David Corbin and his concept of 'Illuminate' from the first moment I heard him speak about it. I have seen the successful results of its implementation numerous times within his clients and mine. More importantly, I have seen even more people and businesses **fail**, because they were not aware of the concept, didn't practice the principles behind it, or were so committed to the idea of *'accentuate the positive', they couldn't relate to it*. David, thank you for bringing us out of the darkness . . . ILLUMINATE!!"

—Phil Wexler, author of *The Quest for Quality, Non-Manipulative Selling*

"David Corbin provides us with the practical and inspiring formula: Acknowledge the 'positive potential' + Understand the 'wisdom from the negative' = Move forward into the 'Illuminated Life'. This is a simple and yet deep reminder of the daily awakenings that can bring harmony and success to our lives."

—Don Campbell, author of *The Mozart Effect* and
   The Harmony of Health

"Stand on your head when you read this book. It's completely counter-intuitive and refreshingly anti-politically-correct. It'll turn your thinking upside-down. We all need David Corbin's shake-it-up approach to questioning what we think we know. He's a renegade, and it turns out . . . he's right! This crisp book is a digestible parable with a point that'll quickly quench your curiosity. There's no wading through a prose-heavy parable. He gets to the point, makes it, and leaves you with a distinctly delighted feeling because it's such a fun read with a pithy purpose."

—George Walther, Hall of Fame Speaker and author of
   What You Say Is What You Get

"Read David Corbin's book about 'Illuminating the Negative'. Once you start applying David's principles, you'll start winning gold medals both professionally and personally."

—Ruben Gonzalez, Three-time Olympian and
   author of *Becoming Unstoppable*

"*Illuminate* will change the way you think. The author, David Corbin, offers practical advice that is based on psychologically sound principles. Readers will understand how avoiding the negative is negative. Corbin's simple 3-step process for dealing with a problem—to recognize, understand, and correct it—is a simple and effective strategy for success in business and in life."

—Paula Schnurr, PhD, author of *Trauma and Health: Physical*
   Health Consequences of Exposure to Extreme Stress

"In talking about the positive power of negative thinking, David Corbin means that one should identify the key road blocks in a business system and come up with sustainable solutions. The main message in *Illuminate* for me was that in order to grow a business one must first identify the key problems inhibiting business growth and then devise robust solutions to overcome those identified deficiencies. In short, find the negatives and turn them into positives."

—Dr Peter C Farrell, founder and Executive Chairman, ResMed Inc.

"The idea of 'Illuminating the Negative' is long overdue. David Corbin has created exceptional results with this model with people at all levels of development and now offers it to the world in a fast, easy to read allegory. It should be read by everybody who wants to learn, grow and flourish."

—Greg Reid, co-author of *Think and Grow Rich, Three Feet from Gold.*

"*Illuminate: Harnessing the Positive Power of Negative Thinking* has a place in every clinician's handbook as an incredibly effective way to approach healthcare, patients, and the personal growth of all healthcare providers. I have used it with my patients and in my own life with excellent results."

—Michael Breus, PhD, The Sleep Doctor author: *Good Night: The Sleep Doctor's 4-Week Program to Better Sleep and Better Health.*

"David Corbin uses the power of storytelling to deliver an excellent concept that will benefit everyone in their business and personal lives. I can't wait to start putting his insights to work."

—Michael Love, President, Nurture by Steelcase

"David Corbin puts an essential new twist on the insight/decision-making process—and he's dead-on. This book will shake-up how you use your own mind at work—and from the shake-up will come breakthroughs. The fact is, we must face reality in business, not hopeful dreams—and then let new insights emerge, based on that reality. David's new book is the golden guide to breakthrough thinking."

—John Selby, author of *Executive Genius* and *Take Charge of Your Mind*

"Excellent! *Illuminate* is not the new age Positive Psychology movement but more in alignment with the research based work of Martin Seligman, PhD, University of Pennsylvania. I read straight through in an hour and 30 minutes and am ready to begin Illuminating my mushrooms!"

—Peter McLaughlin, author of *Catchfire*

"David Corbin's new book *Illuminate* is completely in sync with the challenges that a busy CEO encounters. It offers simple and practical advice. Keeping positive when faced with cutbacks and downsizing requires the Illuminate process. I have heard David speak at conferences around the country and find that he is witty as well as wise, and his new book compliments his thinking processes in way that will resonate with anyone struggling to find answers in the business world."

—Ron Richard, CEO, Sequal Technologies, Inc.

"In a world stressfully focused on quality improvement and positive thinking, David offers up a simple approach worthy of complex thoughts, even the missteps and stumbles in our lives that need bright illumination if we are to reach our goals and hope to exceed them. We need to view the problems themselves not as something to ignore or hide, but as guides to solutions in our working and personal lives."

—Ted Mazer, MD, Board Certified Otolaryngologist;
  past President, Pacific Foundation for Medical Care;
  and past President, San Diego County Medical Society

"I couldn't put this book down until I was done reading it—it's that Illuminating! When I first saw what this book was about, I could only cringe back in fear and horror! It is so difficult to deal with the negative, I thought, why would anyone actually choose to do it? What I came to realize through David's story is that when you realize that dealing with it is the only way to solve it, and further, putting structure to that process removes the 'horror,' it becomes not only easier, but it can also lead to a more creative and enjoyable work setting."

—Jim Bishoff, Administrator,
  VISION Essentials by Kaiser Permanente

"David Corbin is a genius at revealing the bottom-line of what ails most organizations—the inability to face the real problems that real people experience in their efforts to move the organization forward. *Illuminate: Harnessing the Positive Power of Negative Thinking* does just that—it gives us the courage to face the issues and the formula to solve them. Thank God common sense is still the best medicine. Its simple truth is healing!"

—P.S. Perkins, Founder, Human Communication Institute,
  LLC and author of *The Art and Science of Communication:*
  Tools for Effective Communication in the Workplace

illuminate

Harnessing the Positive Power
of Negative Thinking

DAVID M. CORBIN

WILEY

John Wiley & Sons, Inc.

Library of Congress Cataloging-in-Publication Data:

Corbin, David M., 1952-
  Illuminate : Harnessing the positive power of negative thinking / by David M.
Corbin.
    p. cm.
  ISBN 978-0-470-45587-6 (cloth)
  1. Success in business. 2. Negativism. 3. Creative ability in business.
I. Title.
  HF5386.C788 2009
  650.1—dc22   2009000838

Printed in the United States of America

10 9 8 7 6 5 4 3 2 1

Dedicated to

Eleanore Dobbins Corbin

1923–2008

Forever in My Heart

Contents

SECTION 3: FIX IT 99

Foreword

HARRY PAUL

CO-AUTHOR OF *FISH! A REMARKABLE WAY TO BOOST MORALE AND IMPROVE RESULTS, REVVED!,* AND *INSTANT TURNAROUND!*

At first glance, it seems logical. If it's bad, doesn't work, or is a challenge . . . just ignore it. By ignoring the negative, we mistakenly think we have more time and energy to focus on the positive. Makes perfect sense, right? Not really!

In this groundbreaking book, *Illuminate: Harnessing the Positive Power* of *Negative Thinking,* David Corbin takes the position of contrarian and implores us to look at what's not working, broken, or wrong and shed some light on it.

Ignoring what's negative doesn't make any sense. We've heard it growing up: "learn from your mistakes." And we should and need to do this in the workplace. Perhaps without consciously realizing it, the power of *Illuminate* has always been a part of our lives. In science, Thomas Edison was admonished for trying over 300 different ways to make a light bulb. He was reminded constantly about how many times he failed. His response was "I now know over 300 ways not to make a light bulb." David explains that "he illuminated the negative in a positive light and now we have light where there once was darkness." In politics, Senator Robert F. Kennedy said, "There are those that look at things the way they are, and ask why? I dream of things that never were, and ask why not?" Today Barack Obama is President of the United States. These are all examples of looking at what is wrong, understanding the problem, and making action-based decisions that will start us off in the right direction.

The initial feedback on my book, *FISH! A Remarkable Way to Boost Morale and Improve Results,* was that you can't ask people to come to work and have fun. My coauthors and I asked "why not?" Seven million copies later we know we are right. We put the positive power on negative thinking to the test. We found that people did want to come to work and have fun, and that having fun helped get the job done better. Now millions of workers the world over are enjoying work more and being more productive. This kind of paradigm shift is part of the power of *Illuminate*.

When you illuminate your challenges with the three step process, as set out in this book, you are certain to make the most of every situation; positive or negative. The *Illuminate* process actually provides you with more avenues to foster positive energy, discover creative solutions, avoid unwanted "surprises," and help you to achieve and sustain success.

—Harry Paul

Preface

I've never been a traditional thinker. This, I believe, is the secret to the success I have enjoyed for over 30 years as a businessman, entre- preneur, and consultant. But I can understand if you read the subtitle to this book and thought it sounded a little strange, a little scary. Harnessing the positive power of negative thinking? Is he for real?

I want you to know that, yes, I'm for real. And the countless other managers and business owners I've worked with and shown how to Illuminate will assure you that I'm for real, too. The improve- ments they've seen within their companies after they've illuminated the negative is all the proof they need.

The path that led to the creation of this book has been an interesting one. It's ironic that I've made it my life's work to solve business problems and improve workplace environments. In fact, there was a time when I considered *business* a dirty word. Back in the late 1960s, I was a tie-dyed-in-the-wool hippie.

No way was I going to become a cog in the corporate wheel—I was going to help people. I studied and became a counseling therapist in community crisis intervention. This branch of mental health uses psychological techniques to help people communicate better, resolve conflicts, and achieve insight into what's causing their problems. Then, armed with little more than a youthful sense of righteousness, I left that field and my native New York to attend Stanford Medical School. It didn't take long for me to realize that I wasn't cut out to be a modern MD.

Now, fortunately, it didn't take long for me to understand that my hostility toward businesses and the people who make them run was nothing more than prejudice. I still wanted to help people, though, so I got a job in sales, and then I became a sales and marketing trainer and consultant. In doing so, I discovered that my experience in counseling therapy gave me an extraordinary edge when it came to creating and growing a business. I had never taken a business class, but my expertise in the workings of the human mind and behavior allowed me to find new ways to relate to customers and clients.

The first time I used negative thinking, I didn't even know I was doing it. Here's a good example.

The military is required to spend a certain amount of money per year with women- and/or minority-owned businesses. But in 1982, minority- and/or women-owned suppliers of products and services useful to the military had no easy way to get themselves noticed by military buyers. And military buyers had no easy resource telling them which minority- and/or women-owned businesses offered the supplies or services they needed. I tried to suggest to a directory publisher that there was an opportunity here if we could solve this problem, but he wasn't interested. His businesses were doing fine—why go looking for problems on purpose? He told me if I was so gung-ho on this idea, I should go for it myself.

So, I did. It took a lot of negative thinking, which forced me to face, follow, and fix some difficult problems: the red tape that often plagues government institutions; the small businesses that had correspondingly small marketing budgets; and the military buyers who were too busy to waste time hunting outside their regular circle of suppliers. But by focusing on the negatives, I was able to see the potential positives. In the end, I created the first directory—a military Yellow Pages—that conveniently listed qualified military suppliers, and specifically noted small minority- and/or women-owned businesses that qualified for federal spending. But a Yellow Pages is just another Yellow Pages. In talking to engineers and others who purchased for military projects, I discovered that each agency had its own database of internal phone numbers. So I petitioned through the Freedom of Information Act to publish an interbase/interagency directory. That directory helped make the Yellow Pages a success by allowing cross-referencing among buyers. Overall, these two directories made millions of dollars and allowed my company to double in size every year for five years.

I continued to think negatively and my business grew. Then I noticed something. My most successful clients—a mortgage company, a printer, and an interior design company—were also thinking negatively to solve problems. Clearly, people like me and the owners of these businesses had a natural negative-thinking ability. I wondered if it would be possible to teach it to others.

At first, I was a spectacular failure. I'd try to explain the positive effects of negative thinking to my clients and meet fierce resistance. Talk about the negative? Are you crazy? By now, too, the Positive Mental Attitude (PMA) movement had gained traction, resulting in a glut of gurus and bestsellers hawking the power of positive thinking. I wondered if I had missed my moment.

Then one day my young daughter Jenna and I were watching that classic film, *Here Come the*

Waves, on television. Bing Crosby started singing in his syrupy voice, "Ac-cen-tchu-ate the positive, eliminate the negative." It hit me that what I'd been trying to explain to people is that the key to success is not eliminating the negative, it's illuminating it! Only by illuminating our problems can we ultimately eliminate them. That's when I became obsessed with creating a structured methodology for people to use. *Illuminate* outlines that methodology in an easy-to-follow, entertaining story.

Illuminating the negative is about questioning authority. It's about being proactive and thinking outside the box. It's about seeing negative issues in a positive light. We don't need more positive thinking. We need critical thinking, analytical thinking, unafraid-to-face-the-truth thinking. This book offers an example drawn from the experiences of countless individuals who have discovered that negative thinking can bring about unparalleled positive results in anyone's work and life.

—David M. Corbin

SECTION 1

Face It

Chapter 1

Trouble

R elieved to be finally on his way, Jon sighed as he settled into the backseat of the yellow taxi. Half smiling, he turned to wave to his wife and nine-year old son, Ben.

Anne's right, he thought, *I should be here for Ben's All Star game; he's the starting pitcher. But I have no choice. This trip might just save my job.*

The last few months had been difficult for Jon. After 20 years of working at Provident Hospital, his promotion to Director of Human Resources should have marked the high point of his career. And at first, it had. Less than a year ago, he initiated a daring new program he called "On a Mission," geared to eliminate certain problems that had long plagued the hospital, such as low morale and high turnover. One of the keys to the program's success was a new mission statement that put patients at the top of the hospital's priorities. At the time, the program sparked a renewed energy and excitement throughout the medical center. In particular, the physicians, nurses, and other medical staff seemed pleased to have received permission to do whatever it took not only to provide the best treatment possible to their patients, but to make their stay comfortable, dignified, and personalized. Jon had received tremendous kudos for his innovative thinking, including a feature in a national business magazine that pegged him one of America's top-ten "Ones to Watch."

Lately, though, enthusiasm for the program was waning. Staff morale, and hospital revenue, were declining rapidly. Turnover was higher than before the program's implementation, and Jon had no idea why. For the first time in decades, the hospital was hit with a malpractice suit. Ultimately, the suit was dismissed but the incident left everyone involved, including Jon, badly shaken. The hospital was in trouble. And if the hospital was in trouble, Jon was in trouble.

"Face it," Donald Olsten, the hospital's president, had told him the day before, "your program is failing. I'm seeing the same old problems all over again."

"I know," Jon quickly interjected, "but I think with a little time and patience . . ."

Donald went on as though Jon hadn't spoken. "I was hoping to explore solutions during the annual executive retreat, but now I have to attend an emergency meeting of the board. Normally I'd send the Executive VP," he looked away from his computer and directly at Jon, "but considering it was at your insistence that we adopt this new program, it seems to me that it's up to you to find a way to make it work. Otherwise, we'll have to start considering layoffs. I'm sending you on the retreat in my place. That's not a problem, is it?"

Jon knew that it would, in fact, be a problem, considering the last-minute nature of the trip. But he simply nodded and started making plans to leave the next day.

Then, out of nowhere, a thought hit him like a ton of bricks: *Oh, my goodness. Donald was interviewing for an executive position here and we don't have any openings budgeted. Oh no!* He felt his face flush, his pulse elevate, and the thump, thump, thumping of his heart as he considered the possibility that Donald was interviewing for his replacement.

Jon felt a huge storm of fear and betrayal. *I couldn't have put more of myself into this job if I did nothing else in my life. How could they do this to me? What am I going to do? Who can I talk with about this? At this point, I don't know who my friends are or whom I can trust.*

His wife, Anne, was furious when he came home and told her he was leaving. "Again?" she stormed, "You just got back from that conference in Georgia. And what about the opening?"

Jon winced. Before she had decided she needed to spend more time with their son, Anne had been the director of a prominent art gallery in town. Eager to put her professional experience to good use, for the past two years she had volunteered

7

Trouble

countless hours as an art buyer and consultant for the new children's hospital. The grand opening was that Friday.

Anne pursed her lips. "I know you didn't ask for this, but I feel like you never say no to anyone but Ben and me. No matter what the hospital asks of you, you agree to it. All day, all night, sometimes weekends, too. Try to understand, I've worked hard for this. It's a major media event, and I want you to be there with me."

"I know, Anne. The timing is terrible. But Donald is right, the program is my baby. I'm the reason we implemented it at the hospital. No one knows it better than I do, and it makes sense for me to be the one to fix it. And another thing. . . ." He held his tongue before saying, "My job is so much on the line that Donald is probably inter-viewing my replacement."

Then he said something he wished he could take back. "Besides, my job is the reason you were able to take on this project in the first place. It has to come first."

Anne stood still, pale. Jon had never seen her so angry.

"So, your work is more important than mine, is that it?"

"Well, no, but . . ."

"Please, don't say anything else." She turned to go up the stairs. Over her shoulder, she said,

"You know, it's not just the opening. You're also going to miss Ben's game."

For Jon, facing his young son's disappointment was even more difficult than dealing with Anne's understandable wrath.

"Benny-boy, I'm sorry. You know I wish I could be here for your game. Pitch a good one for me, will you? We'll do something special when I get back, I promise. Whatever you want to do. Okay, buddy?"

His son's silence had said just as much as his slumped shoulders.

In the taxi, Jon sat up straight as he thought to himself, *I'll make it up to them as soon as I get back. Right now, I've got to stay positive and focus. I know I can get the hospital back on track. I have to. I really don't want to get fired.*

With a half hour to go before arriving at the airport, Jon refocused his mind on the upcoming retreat. *A week with a group of the most successful business leaders in America might not be so bad. Maybe their success would rub off on me. Maybe they can help me to find a solution to the hospital's problems.* He closed his eyes and tried not to think about the flight ahead.

Chapter 2

Taking Off

Jon buckled his seatbelt on the plane and pulled out some old notes to review, hoping to keep his mind off the fact that he was trapped in a hunk of metal that would soon be hurtling through thin air thousands of feet above the ground. As he shuffled his papers, the older gentleman next to him smiled genially. *Oh, jeez, I hope he's not going to talk my ear off,* thought Jon grumpily.

"Cal Deere," the man said in a friendly Midwestern twang, sticking out his hand. Never one to be rude, Jon extended his hand and forced a smile. He was surprised to feel calluses in Deere's strong handshake. Impatiently, he released his grip. He didn't have time for small talk. He had big problems to solve.

After a relatively smooth takeoff, the flight attendant passed by with a basket of snacks and both men selected a bag of pretzels. Jon stuffed his in the seat pocket while Cal happily tore open his bag and started to munch. A short time passed in silence until Cal turned to Jon and said, "Pardon me, but aren't you Jon Saunders?" Surprised, Jon looked at Cal.

The older man continued. "Didn't I read about you a while back in a *Business Week* article? Something about a new program you initiated that has all the hospitals in the country rethinking their approach to patient care? You run the hospital?"

Jon was surprised, flattered, and embarrassed. "No, I certainly don't run it. I'd like to think I help to run it. I'm the Corporate Director of Human Resources. I was given the chance to try some new ideas out and they got me . . . us . . . some attention." Jon stopped as he realized that Cal looked vaguely familiar.

"Where are you heading today?" Cal asked.

"My boss couldn't attend an executive retreat and asked me to go in his place."

"Really? I'm heading to one, too. Is yours at the Green River Resort?"

"As a matter of fact, it is." Jon paused again, surrendering to the fact there was no way he'd be able to hide behind his notes for the rest of the flight. "You have me at a disadvantage, uh, Cal. I have a feeling I should know who you are."

"Maybe not." Cal said with a reassuring smile. "I do a bit of farming. I'm only attending because I was at a conference nearby. And I figured what the heck, there is always something new to learn."

Jon suddenly realized Calvin Deere was the legendary founder of MegaAgra—the most successful farming and food distribution syndicate in the world. He was struggling for something to say when Cal let him off the hook.

"Tell me more about your new program."

His notes, and his fear of flying now forgotten, Jon told Cal how he had handled the creation and implementation of "On a Mission." Not wanting to lose Cal's admiration, he emphasized the successes the hospital had experienced with the program. "It's been very exciting to see this thing take off. Everything has been going great."

Cal sipped his drink. "I'm impressed with your ideas," he said. "It must have been difficult to convince your leadership team to agree and let you try them."

Before Jon could catch himself, he said, "Convincing the leaders was the easy part. Actually getting all the parts of the program to work the way they're supposed to has been a little harder."

Cal raised an eyebrow. "Oh, I thought everything was going great?"

Realizing his mistake, Jon said, "Well . . . it was." Cautious about revealing too much, he explained, "I'm a big believer in PMA—Positive Mental Attitude. In all the years I've been at Provident, I've emphasized that we need to take a positive approach to everything we do, including the way we think. Folding that philosophy into the On a Mission program made sense." He paused, but Cal just nodded, an inscrutable smile playing around his lips. Jon went on.

"Also, we made sure to get people actively involved right from the beginning. You know, by holding town meetings and making the program and the mission statement relevant to the staff's work process and conditions."

"That's always a good idea," Cal answered.

"I thought so, too," said Jon, pleased. "Initially, we got a lot of positive feedback. We saw signs of growth. The program also nipped some chronic problems in the bud, like turnover. Turnover is costly and disrupts the quality of patient care. But recently, we noted that turnover is increasing again."

"*Hmmm,* that's a puzzle." Cal said.

Jon said, "Look, change is always hard. It's inevitable that we'd lose a little momentum after a big surge forward like the one we just experienced. I just need to get it under control."

Cal looked into Jon's eyes, "Inevitable?"

"Absolutely," Jon replied. He didn't like the skepticism in Cal's voice. It was bad enough that his boss was breathing down his neck; did he really need a perfect stranger questioning him, too?

He waited for Cal to offer a reply. None came. Uncomfortable with the silence, Jon offered, "One thing I know we got right is our mission statement."

Cal smiled. "What does it say?"

"The biggest difference between our old mission statement and the new one is that the new one confirms that the patient has to come first. The emphasis was on systems efficiency and continuous improvement—two important areas, and we would never drop those from our mission. The new one emphasizes an awareness that we exist to enhance our patients' health and wellness however we can, create a positive work environment, and be profitable doing it. I think this is a much more positive message."

"Yes, yes, very positive," Cal replied softly, looking down into the ice cubes melting at the bottom of his plastic cup. "It sounds good for your staff."

"They've all told me how great it is," said Jon proudly. "But then, just last week Judy, the head of our accounting division, gave her notice. In her file, I read that she says she feels overworked. I'm surprised, because she's never complained to me, and she was a big champion of On a Mission. I guess she just didn't get it."

"Didn't get what?" asked Cal.

"That we're only as happy in our work as we allow ourselves to be. If she was feeling overworked, she probably needed to delegate more. She should have talked to me about it. This is another problem I'm seeing around the hospital,

17

people blaming others for their mistakes and problems. I've also heard that some people are refusing to do things because it's not officially part of their job. This kind of negativity is harmful and I need to stop it before it spreads," Jon said.

"Stop the negativity. Are you sure you want to do that?" Cal asked.

What a weird question, Jon thought. Out loud, he said, "I have a lot of experience in this area and I've seen how negative thinking hurts productivity. The whole point of the new program was to make people think and work more positively, and it worked!"

"Indeed, it probably did. But it's not working anymore, is it?"

Speechless, Jon marveled at the old man's bluntness.

Cal leaned in toward Jon, his face kind. "Jon, you must think me terribly rude. It's just that I love to problem-solve, and your situation intrigues me. And when you're my age, you don't have time to beat around the bush. I do apologize."

Unable to resist Cal's genuinely apologetic expression, which reminded him of a basset hound he'd had as a child, Jon softened. "It's okay. But believe me, I've given this issue a lot of thought. I'm sure with a little time and a few tweaks the program will do what it's supposed to do."

"Do you have children?" asked Cal.

Jon smiled, curious about where the conversation was going. "Yes, a boy, Ben. He's nine."

"That's a fun age. Enjoy it while it lasts. They grow up too quickly."

Jon thought of how much he loved his son, and wondered if Ben had forgiven him for missing the game.

Cal went on, "If Ben was having trouble with math but was doing great in English, would you spend all of your time helping him with English?"

Jon said, "Of course not. We'd work on math."

"Exactly!" Cal said. "So, if everyone likes your program and it appeared to be working, why do you think that's where the problem lies? Maybe it's something else altogether."

Jon hadn't thought of this. "Something else? The program is the only thing that's changed recently. What else could it be?"

"It's possible your program didn't nip the problems in the bud, as you say, but rather masked them or diverted your attention away from them. I guarantee that if you don't find those hidden problems now, they'll never go away, no matter how good your program is. Positive thinking is great, but it can only go so far. Acknowledge the positive, but don't ignore the negative. It's like having a baby. You can't simply put it down when it starts to fuss. That's exactly when you need to give it the most care and attention."

"So, acknowledge the positive but focus on the negative?" Jon said, still a little confused.

"Yeah, or as I like to say, accentuate the positive, illuminate the negative."

"I've heard that before. Isn't that a song?" asked Jon.

"Yep. Bing Crosby sang it in a movie called *Here Come the Waves*. What a voice! But the original lyrics are 'Ac-Cent-Tchu-Ate the Positive, Eliminate the Negative,'" replied Cal.

"Right. Eliminate the negative. That's what I'm trying to do," said Jon, pleased to find they'd been on the same page all along.

"Well, Jon, I think you'll find that you will never be able to eliminate the negative until you have the gumption to illuminate it first."

Illuminate? thought Jon with surprise. *What's he talking about?* Before he could press Cal for more details, Cal pulled out a paperback novel from his duffel bag.

"I know you're skeptical, Jon. Do me a favor, give the idea some thought. Consider what it means to illuminate something rather than eliminate it. The difference can be astounding. In the meantime, do you mind if I read my book? Last night I got to a really good part and I can't wait to get back to it. We've got plenty of time to talk at the retreat."

Jon nodded, relieved that the conversation was over. *What a character,* he thought as he reached for his bag of pretzels. *He doesn't know what he's talking about, but he's an interesting old bird.* He didn't feel like looking over his notes any more, but he hadn't brought along anything else to occupy his time. Anne usually bought him something fun to read before a trip. He turned to the window and thought about his wife.

"I think you'll find that you will never be able to eliminate the negative until you have the gumption to illuminate it first."

Chapter 3

First Impressions

J on lost track of Cal in the bustle of getting off the plane and finding his luggage at the airport. Scanning the baggage claim area one last time to see if he could spot the old man, Jon made his way to the taxi queue and found a cab waiting for him. They sped off to the Green River Resort.

Arriving at the historic hotel, Jon appreciatively took in the elegant and luxurious surroundings. *So this is how the big bosses travel,* Jon grinned to himself. *I could get used to this.* A bronze plaque on the lobby wall indicated the building was erected in the late nineteenth century. In keeping with the architecture of the period, the hotel was furnished with polished antiques and decorated with rich fabrics and historic paintings. Jon loved antiques. Early in their marriage, he and Anne would spend weekends scouring antique shops. He missed those days. Anne would love this place.

He called home as soon as he arrived in his room, kicking off his shoes and stretching out on the bed in his dress socks. Anne didn't say much as he described the resort. "There's a curio cabinet downstairs that reminds me of the one we loved so much at that shop in Vermont, but was too big for the car. Remember that? And my room has a great private patio outside the French doors. You'd love it."

First Impressions

Jon realized he was talking too fast, but Anne's silence made him nervous. "Sounds nice," she finally said. "Ben's game went well, too. He pitched five innings and got the win, in case you're interested."

Ouch. Jon could hear it now, loud and clear. Anne was still angry with him. Yet there was no point in arguing in the few minutes he had left before orientation. He replied with forced cheer. "Of course I'm interested. That's great. Tell him I said congratulations!"

"*Mmm-hmm,* " was all he heard back.

Anne clearly needed another day or two to calm down. "Tell Ben I want to hear all about the game when I get home. I'll call you tomorrow."

"You do that," Anne said quietly.

Jon hung up and looked at his cell phone. "One problem at a time," he said to the empty room.

Turning his mind to the retreat, he picked up the rich maroon leather folder. Embossed on the front were the words:

Strategic Leadership: Doing More with Less

He read each of the participants' biographical sketches. On short notice, they had been able to include his on a small square of paper clipped to the bio page. Though he wasn't as high up in the corporate stratosphere as most of the other attendees, Jon's bio held its own. In fact, he thought he came across as a pretty successful, influential man. Anne may be angry with him right now, but the sacrifices he had made had paid off. *You'd never be able to tell my job is on the line,* he thought grimly.

He skimmed the first page of the section labeled "Orientation" for the event's location. Besides informing him that he was to convene in the Wildflower Salon, it also included the following instructions:

Face the challenge: Define the single most important problem you'd like to solve during this retreat.

Cal's voice suddenly sprang into his head. *Illuminate the negative. Well, Cal,* he thought, *I couldn't even if I wanted to. I don't know where to start.*

Changing into a fresh shirt, he tried not to feel nervous meeting some of the most brilliant minds in the corporate world. Maybe they could help him. *Who knows, maybe I can help them,* he grinned to himself. *Why not? I'm "One to Watch." That's got to count for something.* Leaving his problems at home behind, he closed the door and left for the orientation.

27

Jon's bravado wavered as he walked into the elegant salon. All around him were serious people wearing expensive dark suits marred only by white identification badges, chatting in small groups. Glancing around the room, Jon spotted a tall, salt-and-pepper-bearded man sipping a glass of water near one of the tables. Squinting, Jon saw that his name tag identified him as Will Franklin, Executive Vice President of Dobbins Venture Capital. Jon's boss, Donald, had mentioned that Will would be at the retreat, and that it wouldn't hurt for Jon to get to know him. *I wonder what he's got to do with the hospital?* Jon thought. He gathered up his courage and started to move in Will's direction when his path was blocked by a thin, distinguished-looking man.

"I don't believe we've met. I'm Vahe Ramesh of TS&S Laboratories," the man said in a melodic Indian accent.

Jon shook his hand and the two exchanged pleasantries. As they spoke, he inadvertently caught the eye of a redhead speaking animatedly with her hands. She abruptly broke off her conversation with the two other women.

"Lois Signorelli," she said, offering a confident handshake and a brilliant smile. Before the men could introduce themselves, a waiter came to take their drink orders. Ready for a stiff scotch, Jon turned and helped himself to a couple of stuffed mushrooms while he waited for Lois to place her order. "Bourbon on the rocks" she said. Jon thought he noted Vahe cast a disapproving glance in her direction. When it was his turn, he ordered a ginger ale.

Without missing a beat, Lois turned away and resumed her conversation. Suddenly, Vahe and Jon were joined by Will Franklin.

"Vahe, it's good to see you again. How are you?" Will said, ignoring Jon.

Vahe smoothly gestured toward Jon. "I'm doing great. Will, I'd like you to meet Jon Saunders from Provident Hospital."

Will disinterestedly shook Jon's hand and continued, "Let me ask you something, Vahe. Would you agree with me that objective, measurable results are a key business objective?"

Vahe frowned. "Well, yes, but I think in certain circumstances . . ."

"I knew you would," interrupted Will. "All these people trying to get me to invest in their new performance programs, and not one of them with the numbers to prove they work." He shook his head.

Eager to participate, Jon piped up, "Are you looking at the right numbers?"

Will looked at Jon for the first time. "Excuse me?"

Jon flushed. "Are you looking at the right numbers? Are you looking exclusively at profit and loss, or are you checking how many sick days are called in, or whether there has been a decrease in accidents on the factory floor?"

Will looked as though he were about to reply when Lois moved in on his other side. "Lois!" Will exclaimed as though greeting an old friend. "How are you? How's that . . . what do you call it . . . 'Facebook experiment' going?"

Lois's good-natured laugh rang out. "Will, you're showing your age. It's not an experiment, it's called 'social networking' and it's opened up huge branding opportunities for our company. I'll give you all the details, but first, I want to hear about . . ."

The two wandered off. Vahe turned to Jon with a gentle smile.

"I'm impressed. Not many people challenge Will Franklin."

Again, Jon flushed. "I didn't mean to challenge him. I just wanted to talk."

"Will you excuse me?" Vahe asked quickly. "I hate to interrupt, but I just spotted someone I need to speak with before orientation begins. We'll talk again soon, yes? It's been a pleasure."

With that, Vahe left Jon standing alone in the middle of the room. Looking around, he saw Cal Deere sitting at a table with an eggroll in hand, and talking with a young man. Cal's presence at the retreat puzzled Jon. Compared to the other attendees, he seemed over the hill. Even his suit, a standard combination of blue jacket, red and blue tie, white shirt, and khakis, made him look old-fashioned and unsophisticated. He made no effort to mingle. Rather, as far as Jon could tell, Cal had stayed in his seat, observing from afar but warmly greeting anyone who approached him. As Jon got closer, he heard Cal say, ". . . illuminate the negative."

Before Jon could join in, the retreat facilitator, Professor Lynne Bailey, asked everyone to take their seats. As he headed to his chair, he realized that no introductions would be necessary as he'd already met everyone assigned to his table: Lois Signorelli, Vahe Ramesh, Cal Deere, and Will Franklin.

It turned out his seat was next to Cal's. Will was at the opposite side of the table, next to Lois. *Great,* he thought unkindly, *she's next to Will and I'm next to Old MacDonald.*

Chapter 4

Embracing the Message

P rofessor Bailey welcomed the attendees. "Good evening. To those of you who are new to this retreat, I hope you'll take me seriously when I say that we are determined to make your time with us as thought-provoking and productive as possible. So let me or anyone on the retreat staff know if there is something you need or would like to see addressed. I'm delighted to see some familiar faces in the room. It means we've been doing something right all these years."

She went on to explain that the week had been organized to maximize collaboration and interaction among the participants. She described the various seminars that would be offered, and the resources at the executives' disposal.

She hastened to add, "There's one thing we need to accomplish this evening before we head our separate ways. You received a form in your conference folder asking you to answer the question, 'What is the single most important problem you'd like to solve?' If you haven't filled it out already, I'd like you to do so now. When you're done, leave it on this table." She gestured to the empty table nearest to the podium. Jon opened his folder and pulled out the form.

Professor Bailey went on. "After I collect your answers we'll take a fifteen-minute break and then reconvene. After that, you'll have the rest of the evening to yourselves."

Jon looked down at his blank form, and the answer came to him in a sudden flash. He smiled to himself. He had a problem to solve, maybe even more than one, but ultimately the reason he wanted them solved was to preserve the positive gains brought about by his On a Mission program, gains that would help uphold the hospital's mission and values.

After turning in his form, he went outside to get a breath of fresh air. Cal was sitting silently on the patio taking a puff of cherry tobacco from his pipe. Looking up, he invited Jon to sit down.

"You look deep in thought. I don't want to interrupt," Jon replied.

"By all means, park yourself right here." Cal slapped the chair next to him. "Just indulge in a moment of reflection. Every evening, I take a few minutes to look back on my day. I try to embrace all of it, the good and the bad. Especially the bad. It's reassuring and inspiring."

Surprised, Jon said, "I don't understand how focusing on your problems can be reassuring, let alone inspiring. Don't you think it would be healthier to focus on the things that went well during your day? Positive thinking—that's what gives us the confidence to solve our problems. As I always say, 'The glass is half-full.'"

"Well, as I always say, 'If it ain't broke, don't fix it.' That leaves me a lot of time to spend with what's broke."

Jon fought the urge to roll his eyes in exasperation. "Oh, yes, I forgot. Focus on the negative."

"I like to call it 'Illuminate the Negative.' Sounds more positive."

"You got me," Jon chuckled.

"You know, Jon, there's nothing wrong with having a positive mental attitude. But our obsession with it has done everyone a disservice."

"Really? How so?" asked Jon.

"Too many business leaders used the PMA message to justify building a culture that allows people to share only positive thoughts, feelings, and observations. There's no room for disagreement, no room for expressing dissatisfaction without repercussions."

"Well, Cal, that's a bit of an exaggeration. Take my On a Mission program, for instance. Our insistence on taking the positive approach encourages accountability. It doesn't do anyone any good to sit around complaining all day. If you've got a problem and you want me to do something about it, you'd better have an idea for a solution.

It's not fair to expect me to do all your thinking for you. You know your own job requirements better than anyone."

Cal replied, "A leader needs to lead, and sometimes that means carrying more than your own load."

Jon shook his head. Cal was clearly from the old guard and wasn't up on the latest research. "Leaders need to encourage leadership in others, Cal. Carrying someone else's load doesn't help them—it makes them weak. And I can't afford to have weaklings on my staff. I've got my own job to take care of, I can't do everyone else's, too."

Cal sighed. "You're hard on people, Jon."

"I don't think so," Jon said defensively. "I'm very concerned with my staff's wellbeing." He pressed his hands over his eyes in frustration. "Do you know that my boss is threatening layoffs if I can't fix the problems at the hospital? That's the worst solution I can imagine, and I'll do anything I can to prevent it."

"Now you're talking sense," said Cal.

"I'm glad you agree. But Cal, that doesn't mean I'm going to coddle my staff. No one gave me a break when I was coming up the ranks. I had to think for myself, solve my own problems. I didn't whine and complain. I stayed positive and proactive and took responsibility for my actions. That's how I got to where I am today."

Cal turned to Jon, "Right. But tell me, what would you do if someone came into your office and said, 'I smell smoke?'"

Jon drew his eyebrows together, puzzled. *What was the old guy driving at?* "I'd look around for the source of the fire and try to put it out."

"Right. But that's not what's happening at your hospital. The fire is there, and everyone can smell it, but they're all afraid to yell 'I smell smoke!' for fear of being branded a pessimist or a complainer. And what's the smart thing to do if you smell smoke but can't talk about it?"

Jon hesitated before speaking. "Leave."

Cal looked out over the patio balcony, "I think you might have just illuminated your turnover problem."

Cal had a point, thought Jon.

"Too many business leaders used the PMA philosophy in a way that allowed no room for discussion of challenges, issues, concerns, or shortcomings without fear of being labeled contrary or negative."

"I'd like to think I've built a good rapport with my staff, and that they feel comfortable coming to me when there's something important to discuss," he said weakly.

Cal continued to gaze out over the balcony. "I haven't known you long, but I'm willing to bet your staff does like you. Sometimes it's precisely because of good rapport that problems go unsolved."

Jon had never heard this train of thought before. "Go on."

"Rapport is vital to interpersonal relations. It takes a tremendous amount of trust to put that rapport at risk, to jeopardize a good relationship by bringing up things no one really wants to talk about. And it takes even more courage to do that in a business relationship where power—how much a person has over you, how much you have over a person—comes into play."

Jon thought about his relationship with his boss. How long had he waited to talk to Donald about the hospital's problems? Too long, for fear of what his boss would say. How many other people had done the same thing? What about Judy, the head of Accounting, who had resigned without warning?

Cal puffed on his pipe. "Like mushrooms, problems grow best in the dark. If you want to figure out your problems, you have to be brave

41

Embracing the Message

enough to shine a light on them—a positive light, but a light nonetheless—and you have to be brave enough to let others shine a light on them, too."

Confident the growing darkness wouldn't betray him, Jon now did roll his eyes.

Cal took another puff on his pipe and said, "I'm old, Jon, but I'm not blind. I see you rolling your eyes over there. You think I'm a corny old coot, right?" He sounded amused.

Jon shrugged sheepishly. "I'm sorry, I think we just talk a different language. Let me ask you this: What if I don't know what my problem is? What if I don't even know where to look for those, uh, mushrooms? How am I supposed to figure out what to illuminate?"

"It's a very advanced technique." Cal grinned. "If you want to find mushrooms, you look in the likeliest spots: the darkest, dankest, most mushroom-friendly places you can find. If you want to find your problem, you also look in the likeliest spots."

"Cal, you're losing me here. I'm not a mushroom farmer, I'm a manager."

Cal chuckled. "Okay, back to our advanced technique. Here's what you do: You make a list. You list the most pressing problems you currently have. Then you write down the possible causes of those problems, regardless of whether you have evidence to confirm whether you're right or wrong. Next, you talk to the people most affected by the problems and get their take on it. You add their insight to the list. By combining all of these points of view and experience—yours and your subordinates', and maybe even your superiors'—you should be able to pinpoint the likeliest cause of each problem. Last, you look at the list and ask yourself, 'Which problem can I solve that will fix the most problems at one time?' That's how you know where to begin."

"That's it?"

"That's it. But you'd be surprised at how few people take the time to do it."

Jon said, "Cal, I respect your ideas, I really do. But believe me, a simple list is not going to help me. Can you imagine what would happen if my boss asked me how I intend to fix our problems and I said, 'Let me make a list and I'll get back to you'? No one would take me seriously."

Cal turned to Jon. "Why does it matter what other people think? Why do you young people have to make everything so complicated?"

Jon scratched his head. "I don't know. Because life is complicated?"

Cal sighed. "I can see why you might feel that way, Jon. But when you get to be my age, you'll see that life is really quite simple. Listen. Learn. Illuminate. Trust me. Allowing and fostering negative thinking in a positive light is the most effective way to achieve the results you want in your work and your life."

Jon mused. "To eliminate problems, you have to *illuminate* problems."

"And to illuminate problems, you have to create a safe problem-solving environment," added Cal.

Lois suddenly leaned out the door, "Excuse me, we're about to start again. I didn't want you to miss anything."

"Thanks!" called out Cal with a wave. To Jon, he said, "I enjoyed this talk."

Jon replied, "I enjoyed it, too." He was surprised to realize that he meant it.

* * *

"Nowhere in the Positive Mental Attitude philosophy does it say to ignore the negative issues and factors."

As they wove their way back to their seats, Professor Bailey was already speaking. "I've reviewed your responses to the question you see on the overhead."

Sure enough, behind her was now a glowing screen that read:

What is the single most important problem you'd like to solve?

"Although each of your answers differed, there were commonalities that I took the liberty of rewording and combining into three overarching themes. Therefore, at this point, we can safely say that everyone in this room is struggling with one or more of these three major problems."

With one click of the mouse, the projector screen blinked and switched to a new page, where Professor Bailey had written down three numbered points. Jon was both pleased and embarrassed to see a version of his "single most important problem" included:

- Keeping current with trends of today while creating new ideas for tomorrow.
- Living the company's mission and values in the face of fierce competition and rapidly evolving conditions.

- Balancing the influence of statistics and in-the-trenches experience when setting policy.

"Each of you should benefit from examining these issues, even if they don't directly relate to the specific problem you're dealing with right now. Get to know the people sharing your table—these are also the members of your problem-solving team. It will be up to each team to choose which problem to discuss during the week."

She turned off the projector and raised the lights.

"We've added something new to the program this year. We're having a contest to decide who has developed the most exciting new management theory. For those of you who'd like to participate, write a brief essay explaining the main idea or theory that has been instrumental in your professional success. Your papers are due by the end of Thursday. The retreat staff will review each essay. Each will be judged on four criteria: Is the idea easily understood? Is the idea easily implemented? How sustainable is the idea? And finally: How inspiring is the essay? We'll announce the winner on Friday night. Good luck, and let's have a great time this week."

Embracing the Message

SECTION 2

Follow It

Chapter 5

Seeing the Light

The days passed quickly. Jon began to wonder how he'd ever remember everything he had learned. There were group sessions to address goals, seminars about recent changes in industry, marketing and training sessions, as well as lectures on demographic trends. In the evening, Jon composed his essay, which he had titled *Half Full: The Power of Positive Thinking*, on his laptop. Despite his fatigue and information overload, Jon was having fun.

The exception was during the problem-solving sessions. Jon's team had decided to focus on the second problem: how to stay true to and live the company's values and missions. No one could agree on a way to tackle the thorny issue, though not for lack of trying. Jon did his best to agree with Will whenever possible in the hopes of fostering a bond with the man, if not a friendship. Will, for his part, didn't seem interested. He was cordial, and actively involved in the group discussion, but as soon as they adjourned he'd leave without a backward glance. Jon still had no idea why his boss thought Will was such an important person to know.

At night, after he'd shut off his laptop and turned out the light, Jon allowed himself to think about Anne. He still had not called her, though he knew he should. Every day he sat on the edge of the bed and tried to muster the courage to call, but his nerve failed him. He'd spoken several times to Ben on Ben's phone, the one with only three buttons for calling Mom, Dad, or 911. He knew things were running smoothly at home and that Ben, in typical Ben fashion, had already forgiven him for not being there for his big game. But every time he started to dial Anne's number, he snapped the phone shut before he could finish. He just couldn't face another fight. Maybe a cooling-off period would be good for them. Hadn't he read somewhere that couples shouldn't argue in the heat of the moment? Still, he was worried. He checked his messages regularly. And there were none from Anne.

Each morning Jon looked forward to his nightly meeting with Cal. They met on the patio where Cal had gone that first evening for his reflection time. Cal and Jon didn't always see eye to eye, but their debates were good natured and stimulating.

One evening was particularly beautiful. The reds and oranges of the sunset were spectacular and the two men spent a few minutes taking in the view. Cal broke the silence. "How's the essay coming along?"

Jon gladly replied that he had finished it. He told Cal, "Basically, I described the steps we used in creating and implementing the On a Mission program. Happily we created simple steps for all to remember—and they worked well in the essay."

Jon paused and said, "You know, Cal, I've got to say that while the program has its problems, I still consider it a success. We did experience positive indicators early on and I know we're onto something there."

"Those positive results are the very reason why you should consider it a success," Cal replied. "But have you given any more thought to what's going wrong?"

"I do nothing *but* think about it, but I can't figure it out."

"You said turnover is a problem, right?"

"Cal, I read the exit interviews. Everyone says they're happy. I can't counter every job offer with a raise and more vacation. We're financially strapped as it is."

"Everyone says they're happy, eh?"

"Yes."

"If they were happy, they wouldn't leave, plain and simple. Happy people don't abandon their jobs."

Jon thought about this for a while. The sun was almost set when he finally said, "Maybe I've kept the hospital's problems in the dark because I didn't want to admit that the new mission program couldn't fix everything. Maybe it's not just the

55

Seeing the Light

new program that needs to be illuminated; maybe I need to illuminate the whole hospital."

Cal smiled. "You just took the first step to eliminating your problems," he said tapping his pipe against his chair.

"There are steps?"

"Yep. Three of 'em."

"Were you planning on telling me?"

"I didn't tell you earlier? Are you sure?" Cal scratched his cheek. "I could have sworn I did. They're very simple, you know. You could have figured it out yourself."

"Humor me."

Cal stood and stretched.

"Face it, follow it, fix it. Illuminate the problem so you can eliminate it. It's that simple."

"It is?"

"It is. Now, I'll see you in the morning." Then Cal ambled back inside.

Jon blurted out, without reservation and completely uncensored, "Cal . . . wait . . . please—I really need those steps so I can keep my job!"

Cal stopped, turned toward Jon, and with compassion in his eyes and voice said, "Jon, I'm very happy to share them with you but I'm too tired just now. Let's talk tomorrow."

"Just a quick overview in the time it takes for me to walk you back to your room, okay?"

Three Steps To Illuminate

Face It

Follow It

Fix It

"All right then, just till we get to my room. As I told you, the three steps are 'Face It, Follow It, and Fix It.' I'll give you a couple of sentences about each to chew on. Let's start with 'Face It.'"

"*Facing it* is a classic example of the proverbial *simple but not easy* process. I've seen many a case of managers not taking seriously the observations of staff—sort of staying in denial because they don't immediately agree with the feedback."

"You mean that the managers dismiss the input because they aren't yet aware of the problem?" Jon responded.

"You got it. This can be challenging for people because it seems to be human nature to resist input when you don't actually believe that there *is* a problem. It takes courage and conviction to allow oneself to be open minded, flexible, present, and vulnerable. *Facing it* is not for the weak and timid, and certainly not for those who are unwilling or unable to accept total personal responsibility. I mean, you've got to put your face forward, point your nose and eyes right in the face of the issue, and be willing to really see what's there. So, the first step is to Face It."

Cal quickly added, "Then, you Follow It. That's step number two. And what we do here in Follow It is to clearly define the challenge. Then, like that television show—what's it called, *Crime Investigators?*"

"Oh, you mean *CSI*? It's called *Crime Scene Investigators*."

"Exactly. The next step in Follow It is just like what those investigators do. Ask yourself the probing questions like, where does this challenge reside, who is affected, what is keeping this challenge alive, who or what is feeding it, and questions like that. I've learned through the years that Follow It is the key to Illuminating. I say that because it's where you gather information that otherwise goes undetected and unaddressed and will bite you in the 'you-know-what' if you *don't* Follow It," chuckled Cal.

"And that's where you eliminate the challenge, right?" asked Jon.

"Yes and no. See, Jon, if you eliminate the challenge too soon, and by that I mean without understanding the origin, impact, and the like, then you will probably just make a short-term fix. Back home, we say, 'If you don't pull it out by the roots, it's just a matter of time until it pops back up.'"

Enthusiastically Jon agreed and confirmed, "Got it. Face It and then Follow It before you Fix It."

"Exactly. Face It, Follow It, and Fix It . . . in that order. You see, so many people skip the Follow It stage."

"Is that because they don't have the time to follow it and investigate it?" Jon asked quickly, as he was mindful that they were almost at Cal's room and his lesson might end abruptly.

"Yes, time is a factor because there is a tendency among high achievers to want to fix it and move on." Cal responded.

Jon thought to himself how many times he'd been part of the quick-fix solutions at the hospital and how they tended to resurface shortly after. Wanting to agree with Cal and offer these confirming examples, Jon caught himself and, in the interest of time, simply asked, "Will you please review the Fix It stage for me?"

"Yes. Fix It. Do what it takes to eliminate the causes of the challenge, the contributing factors that keep that challenge alive, and then either eliminate those causes and factors or at least minimize their impact. That process, getting to work on the findings of step two, Follow It, is the essence of Fix It. That's step three and, when you do the steps in order, then Fix It has a better chance of sustaining the 'fix.' Does that make sense?"

"Cal, it makes perfect sense to me. I know it's late and your room is just around that corner, so I will just say this: Thank you, thank you, and thank you. This is simply brilliant and brilliantly simple. We can do these three steps, I know we can. Good night, Cal, and please know that you've interrupted my sleep pattern for a couple of days because I can't imagine my being able to sleep tonight!"

"Well, pace yourself, young man; we've got a lot of work ahead of us. Good night."

"Good night," Jon said, putting his hand out for a deeply sincere handshake.

Face It

"Be willing to put your face forward, open your eyes and ears and especially your mind . . . and consider the validity of observations even if you don't immediately agree. Be open, courageous, and allow for a 'beginners mind.'"

Follow It

"Ask yourself the probing questions, such as:

> Where does this challenge reside?
>
> Who is affected?
>
> What is keeping this challenge alive?
>
> Who or what is feeding it?"

Fix It

"Do what it takes to eliminate or at least minimize the cause(s) and contributing factor(s) that keep that challenge alive."

Chapter 6

Spreading the Word

O n Friday, the final day of the retreat, Jon awoke more rested than he had felt all week. After turning on the coffee pot, he showered and shaved, whistling the Bing Crosby tune that he couldn't get out of his head. Then, armed with a renewed optimism and a steamy cup of strong coffee, he called home.

"Hi, it's me!" he said as warmly as possible, trying to ignore his fluttering stomach.

"Oh, hi." Anne replied.

She sounds tired, Jon thought. "How's everything going? How's Ben?" he asked, keeping his voice upbeat.

"Ben is fine. He has a dentist appointment this morning and a ball game tonight."

"Good, good. This retreat has had us hopping." He paused, and then he softened his tone. "I'm sorry I haven't called. I wanted to, I really did. I just thought maybe we should cool off a bit before talking again. I didn't want to fight."

"Well, maybe that was a good idea," Anne said. He waited for her to go on. When she didn't he quickly interjected, "Okay . . . well, I'm glad that's out of the way. Listen, the weather is supposed to be good so I shouldn't have any trouble with the flight home."

"That's good. I'll be there to pick you up on time, don't worry." Was that forced cheer in her voice? "I've got to go. I want to make sure Ben brushes his teeth."

She's busy, I caught her at a bad time, Jon thought. "Okay, well, make sure you tell him his dad said hi, too, and I'll see him tomorrow."

"I'll do that, Jon," and she hung up the phone. It took Jon a second to realize that she hadn't said goodbye.

* * *

The dining room was buzzing with people by the time Jon arrived for breakfast. He looked around and found his group at their usual table. As he headed to his seat, Jon overheard Lois tell Will, "I guess we'll just have to admit defeat."

Vahe sat next to her, slowly chewing his granola as he listened intently, as usual.

"Why, Lois?" asked Jon, sitting down.

"How could you forget? We don't have an answer to the problem we picked—how to stay true to one's mission and values in the face of tough competition."

Jon realized she was right, but he wasn't in the mood for such debates this morning. He looked around for Cal, and noticed the old man was nowhere to be found.

Will sipped his coffee and said, "Lois, give it up. It was an impossible question. No one else will have an answer, either."

Jon looked up.

"Impossible? Why is that, Will?"

Will looked over his coffee cup at Jon. "Look, I've played along because I thought it was a good thought exercise, but the truth of the matter is that every company in the world has the same mission: to make money. You can couch it in all the feel-good language you want, but we're all in business to make money."

Will glanced over at Lois and grinned, "Now, don't go calling me Scrooge, Lois. There's nothing wrong with making money. The more money we make, the more money people who work for us make, which means their families do better, which means they can afford to do better things for the world. Everyone wins." Then he turned to Vahe. "Vahe, surely you'll agree with me that no company can compete in this day and age if they're hung up on such soft-hearted terms like 'values.' It's an empty word."

Suddenly, Jon didn't care that his boss wanted him to get on Will's good side. "It's not an empty word to me," he said quietly.

Will looked over at him.

"Really? Jon, what would you say are the values at Provident?"

"We value the patients and their families. We value lifesaving research and cutting-edge technology. We value compassion. We value our staff."

Will nodded. "That's what I thought you'd say. And I believe you. But I also know for a fact that if the hospital starts to lose money, you're going to lay people off to fix your bottom line. And if you continue to lose money, you'll cut back wherever you have to. It'll be in small ways, things the general public and media won't necessarily have to know about, but every single person who works in that hospital will feel the effects. So ultimately, you're willing to compromise your values in the interest of money."

Jon didn't know what to say. Then he looked over at Cal's empty chair.

Will followed his gaze. "Cal? You're thinking Cal would disagree? Look, Cal is a lovely man, but his time has passed. He built his company during a very different time than the one we're in now. He's obsolete."

"Obsolete? Will, I'm going to prove you wrong," he said, as he pulled a pen from his pocket and started scribbling on his napkin.

Vahe cleared his throat. "Jon, I don't think Will meant anything personal . . ."

Jon looked at Vahe. "No, Vahe, he didn't mean anything personal. But it's gotten personal." He wrote at the top of the napkin:

WHAT ARE THE PROBLEMS?

- Turnover on the rise
- Morale on the decline
- Negative attitudes
- Poor communication

For the first time, Jon actually felt like he was making progress. He didn't have much on paper yet, but now that he had faced the fact that there was a problem, he was ready to find out which one needed his attention most. He wished that Cal would arrive.

Lois spoke first. "Jon, what are you doing?"

Jon sighed, put down his pen and said, "Will has no idea how close to the truth he is. I'll be honest, Provident has problems. We initiated a new program that modified our mission statement, and we implemented the new version of it in every department. It seemed to have the intended effect—higher morale, increased productivity, all that stuff performance programs are supposed to do for a company—but lately we're starting to see old patterns crop up again. It's gotten so bad there's talk of laying people off."

"So, changing your mission statement didn't do any good, it just prolonged the inevitable." Will said gently.

"Laying people off is not inevitable, Will. It's a way of punishing others for management's inability to solve a company's problems. I tried

69

implementing a solution, but it hasn't worked the way I had hoped. Cal helped me to understand that a new system, even a good system, doesn't work unless it fixes the problems that were there to begin with. I've finally faced the fact that those problems exist. Now, I need to get everyone I work with involved in shedding light on them to fix them."

Lois piped up, "I'd be careful about getting your co-workers involved too soon. Talking too much about negative things just brings up a lot of negative attitudes."

Vahe agreed. "You want to focus on the positive, Jon. No one wants to work in a negative environment."

"That's just it," Jon pressed. "You don't deal with the negatives negatively; you put a positive light on them. Cal says we need to 'acknowledge the positive and illuminate the negative.' You illuminate the negative so everyone can see it and work to eliminate it."

"Better you should bring their attention to the problem once you can reassure them you've got a solution in mind. Otherwise, you'll scare everyone," said Will.

"With all due respect, I'm not dealing with children. My staff is made up of mature adults with years of experience. Who's to say they couldn't offer a better solution to the problem than I? That's just it," Jon pressed.

"You don't deal with the negatives negatively; you put a positive light on them. Cal says we need to 'acknowledge the positive and illuminate the negative.' You illuminate the negative so everyone can see it and work to eliminate it."

Jon looked around at the group. "I'm sure Cal can explain this philosophy better than I can. We should ask him about it when he gets here."

At that moment, Professor Bailey stepped up to her podium and tapped on the microphone. "May I have your attention, please?" she announced. "Before we get started, I would like to inform you that Calvin Deere will not be with us today. He was taken to the hospital last night."

Murmurs were heard throughout the crowd, and everyone at Jon's table looked at each other and the empty chair where Cal should have been.

"Apparently he collapsed on the way to his room after dinner." Jon gasped. Cal had given him no indication he didn't feel well. "We've been advised that his condition is not serious, but he will be monitored at the hospital for a couple of days while they perform some precautionary tests. In the meantime, a get-well card is being passed around for you to sign."

Jon was surprised by how worried he was about a man whom he'd known for only a few days.

"Ladies and gentlemen," Professor Bailey continued, "I'd like to move on to some better news. We have a winner for our contest. I'd like to start by telling you how impressed the retreat committee was with the papers. Each of you did an excellent job outlining the strategy behind your success. However, one paper stood out above the rest. It addresses a timeless problem in a simple, easy-to-understand manner, and scored top numbers in all four categories." She chuckled as she continued. "That paper is titled, *Illuminate, or The Hunt for Mushrooms: How Negative Thinking Can Solve Your Problems.* Cal Deere, its author, is unfortunately not here to accept his award, but I trust you will all contact him on your own to congratulate him."

Jon's ears perked up. Well, I'll be. . . . Good for Cal, he thought.

Will whispered, "Jon, is that what you were talking about?"

Before Jon could answer, Professor Bailey moved on to invite the groups to discuss the outcome of their problem-solving exercise. The last group she pointed to was Jon's table. "Okay, let's hear what you came up with."

Jon, Will, and Lois looked blankly at each other. Then Vahe stood up. "I'm afraid that we couldn't agree on a concrete way to preserve a company's values when confronted with stiff competition. In fact, there was some debate about whether company values truly exist at all."

Professor Bailey looked surprised.

Vahe continued, "However, we've just become aware of Cal Deere's Illuminate theory. If it works, it may provide a way for companies to solve their problems in concordance with the values they profess. I, for one, am keenly interested to see how Mr. Deere's theory might be applied in the real world. I'd like to give it a try and let you know how things go at a later date."

Professor Bailey tugged at her jacket. "Well, I don't see why not. You have our e-mail addresses on the participant contact sheet. By all means, let us know what you discover."

As the seminar came to a close, participants were told copies of Cal's winning paper were available for anyone interested.

As people rose to leave, the group sitting at Jon's table seemed reluctant to move. Vahe finally went up to the front of the room and returned with a stack of papers in hand. "I've taken the liberty of getting each of you a copy of Cal's essay."

Jon was excited as he grabbed his copy. If he couldn't talk to Cal, this was certainly the next best thing.

As they rose to leave, everyone shook hands and promised to keep in touch. Will came around to Jon's side of the table, his hand outstretched. To Jon's astonishment, he was smiling.

"Jon, I like your style," he said genially. "I don't always agree with you, but you've got conviction. I admire that in a person."

Jon shook Will's hand and smiled back. "Thanks, Will, that means a lot to me. I hope we'll be able to stay in touch."

"Absolutely," replied Will. "I'll be interested to hear how things develop at the hospital." As Will walked away, Jon sighed with relief. If nothing else, he could tell his boss that venture capitalist Will Franklin liked his style.

Chapter 7

Darkness

J on had read Cal's paper several times already, but once again pulled it out on the plane ride home. He picked up his pencil and started underlining passages that he'd want to highlight when he introduced the *Illuminate* concept to Donald, his boss.

Vahe had gone to the hospital to visit Cal the afternoon before and delivered his award. During the final social hour, Vahe had reassured the group that Cal was tired, but improving.

Before Jon knew it, the flight attendant announced they would be landing soon. He filed his papers neatly and tucked them back in his briefcase before looking out the window at the familiar surroundings of the airport.

As Jon rolled his suitcase out of the baggage area and to the passenger pickup zone, he spotted Anne leaning against the side of their car. She smiled, but Jon wasn't sure it reached her eyes.

He leaned over to give her a quick kiss, catching her cheek. "Hi, hon," he said.

"Welcome back," she said.

Throwing his bag in the trunk, he took a deep breath. There was something stiff about Anne's demeanor, and it made him nervous.

"Anything new?" Jon asked as he settled into the passenger seat.

"Not really," Anne replied, checking the side mirror as she pulled away from the curb.

Well, if she doesn't want to talk about it, I certainly don't, Jon thought. To fill the silence, he told her about the retreat, the people he'd met, and Cal and his sudden illness.

Anne didn't have much to say as Jon talked. She pulled out onto the freeway and paid attention to the road while Jon described in further detail the elegance of the hotel, and how she would have enjoyed the dinner the night before.

"I'm sure I would have. Except I was at the children's hospital opening night gala. I was interviewed by the press. I was on TV."

"That's right, I forgot! You were on TV? Did you tape it?"

Anne almost smiled. "People seemed impressed with how we tried to make each room and each therapy area warm and comfortable, and how the art was so much more stimulating and interesting than the watercolor landscapes you usually find at hospitals."

"I'm sorry I wasn't there, hon," Jon said sincerely. "But you know this was important."

"This was important, too."

Jon sighed. "I never said it wasn't and you know it. Look, let's get past this. How about we go to dinner tomorrow night? Can you find a sitter for Ben?"

"We don't need a sitter. Ben will be with my mom. In fact, we both will."

Jon turned his head to look at Anne. She stared straight ahead, her fingers tightly gripping the steering wheel.

"What's that supposed to mean?" he asked.

"Ben and I will be staying with my mom for a while. I need time to sort out what I want."

"What are you talking about? What do you mean, what you want? You can't move out! I know you're upset, but . . ."

Anne interrupted, "This is not out of the blue. Jon, my feelings and my work and, yes, our family have taken a backseat to your needs and especially your work for a long time. I never thought I could be with someone, yet feel so alone. I've tried to talk to you about it, but you're always wrapped up in the hospital, or preparing for a meeting or some-thing else, and nothing I say seems to register. My feelings have not been important to you at all."

"That's not fair, Anne. I don't think you under-stand how much pressure I've been under lately . . ."

"It's not just lately. You haven't been present for this family for a long time."

"How can you say that? We had a great vacation last year . . ."

"We took four days in Boca and you brought your laptop and phone. And yes, things were good while we were there, but as soon as we got home the same old problems started up again. Do you know you've never once asked me about my work?"

Jon was about to deny her statement but hesitated, afraid it might be true. "Okay, so maybe I've been a little self-involved. But honey, this job is what allows you to do your work, and send Ben to camp, and pay for the house . . ."

"Jon, that's not the issue. I don't even care about the house."

"You love that house!" Jon countered.

"No, Jon, *you* love that house. That's just another example of how little you know me."

"Enlighten me then, Anne. What do you want?"

"That's what I need to figure out, Jon. I need you to give me space so I can." Anne's voice was calm and quiet.

The car pulled into the driveway. They were home. Turning to his wife, Jon said, "Come on, Anne, let's go inside and talk about this."

"Space, Jon. Please give me some space," she said.

"Ben—can I at least talk to Ben?" he asked.

"Of course you can. He wants to talk to you too. I'll have him call you later."

Jon got out of the car, not believing what was happening. He stood in the driveway and watched her drive off. He stood still for so long that the motion-sensored light above the garage winked out, leaving him in total darkness.

Chapter 8

Step by Step

It was a long night. Jon hadn't realized how accustomed he was to noise, noise that sometimes bothered him when he was working in the den, but that was part of the comforting sounds of his home. There was no clatter of dishes while Anne got supper ready. The back door stayed closed and silent—Ben wasn't running in and out like he'd been told countless times not to do. And Jon missed it.

Several times, he picked up Cal's paper and a notepad, thinking he'd take his mind off things by diving into work, but his mind kept returning back to the problem at home. *I can't believe they're gone. Why didn't I see this coming? What could I have done differently? Why is Anne being so unreasonable? She has to know how important my job is to all of us.*

The house was so quiet that Jon jumped when the phone rang around eight o'clock. The first word out of his mouth was, "Anne?"

"No, Dad, it's Ben," chirped the familiar voice of his son.

"Oh, Ben, sorry. I thought it was your mom. How are you doing, Son?"

"Good, Dad. Grandma made cookies with lots of chocolate chips, and tomorrow she's going to take me to practice. And, Dad, she let me make a tent in the basement. You oughta see it, it's so cool."

Laughing, Jon listened to Ben, who couldn't seem to talk fast enough. *He's excited. It's like he's on a little vacation,* he thought.

"I'm sure it's the coolest tent in town, Benny," he said into the receiver. "Why don't you ask your mom and Grandma if it's okay if I pick you up and take you to practice tomorrow? Afterwards, we can go and get an ice cream. How's that sound?"

"That'd be awesome, Dad! Pick me up at two, okay?"

"Sure thing, Son. I'll clear it with Mom, you can count on it. You be a good boy for Mom and Grandma, okay?"

"All right. I gotta go now. Mom says I have to take a shower tonight. Can you believe it?"

Smiling, Jon said, "Yeah, Ben, I can. Better get in there and do it. I'll see you tomorrow."

I miss you so much, Jon thought as he hung up the phone. He gave up on getting any work done and put his papers away. For the rest of the night, he tossed and turned as he thought about Anne and Ben, finally falling asleep around dawn.

The next day, while sipping his coffee, he pulled out Cal's *Illuminate the Negative* paper. He jotted down the steps to the process:

Three Steps to Illumination

- Face It
- Follow It
- Fix It

Jon had gotten past the first step. He'd admitted to himself that there were problems at the hospital that weren't being solved by On a Mission. His only mistake had been to focus almost exclusively on the positive effects of the program and dismiss what wasn't working.

He'd already started step number two. He pulled out the list of problems he had begun at the conference and added to on the flight home:

Problems

- Turnover on the Rise
- Morale on the Decline
- Poor Communication
- Negative Attitudes
- Finger-pointing

Reviewing his list, he lingered over the third item, poor communication. He realized that this was one problem he could solve that would help solve the other problems as well. That was where he was going to start. Then, looking at the time, he scooped up his car keys to go pick up Ben, leaving the sheet of paper with the list of problems on top of his desk—face up.

Chapter 9

Communicating

Jon and Ben had a great afternoon. After Ben's practice, they stopped and got chocolate ice cream, their favorite, then they walked around the park for a while. Jon brought Ben home and they watched a couple of his son's favorite movies. Time flew, and before they knew it, it was time to take Ben back to his grandma's. *This is only temporary,* Jon thought. *It'll work itself out in a day or two.*

Jon spent the next morning catching up on his e-mails and working on his calendar. He needed to set aside time to communicate with the staff to see if they could help him shed light on some of the hospital's underlying problems.

He also made a note to contact Judy, the head of Accounting. It was time for him to learn exactly why she had resigned.

He left her a voice mail, letting her know he wanted a few minutes to speak to her this morning. Then he sent his boss an e-mail letting him know that the retreat had gone well and that he was working on a new concept that would turn things around at the hospital.

As he was hanging up, there was a knock on his door.

Communicating

"Is this a bad time?" Judy asked.

"No, no, not at all. Come in. Sit down." Jon ushered her in.

After pouring them each a cup of coffee, Jon approached the subject of Judy's resignation. "I want to understand the real reasons why you're leaving."

"Well, I got another job offer."

Jon nodded. "Yes, I understand that. But you wouldn't have applied for that other job if you were completely happy here."

"Oh, I've been happy. Really, I've learned a great deal and it's been a challenging experience," Judy said earnestly.

"I'm glad to hear it. But will you do me a favor? Will you think negatively for a minute?"

Judy's hands twisted in her lap. "Think negatively?"

Jon smiled broadly and spread his hands at his side, palms out. "Judy, this isn't a trick! I promise. I really, really want to know why you were dissatisfied here."

It took a few minutes for Jon to convince Judy that she was free, even welcome, to tell him the truth—all of it. He jotted a few notes down as she talked, making a list of whatever positive things she said, as well as the negative. When she was done, he reviewed his notes:

Positives

- Judy is satisfied with her salary.
- Loves living on the West Coast.
- Believes most of the changes brought about by the implementation of On a Mission are good.

Jon paused over the last item. *Most of the changes are good. Not all.* He thought, *A week ago, "most" would have been good enough for me. Not anymore. We'll have to talk about that one further.* He read on:

Negatives

- Aging parents need care—they live 40 miles away and her schedule doesn't allow enough flexibility to tend to them.
- The On a Mission program requires significantly more paperwork from the accounting department.
- Additional resources and budgets were never added to ease the staff's additional workload.

So that's how illumination works, Jon thought. *I've been assuming I knew what Judy's problem was when in fact it's something entirely different. Without illumination, I'd still be in the dark.*

The problem wasn't that Judy wasn't delegating or handling her job responsibilities. The problem was that her job requirement had changed but she hadn't been given the tools to change with it. And that was one problem that had nothing to do with the hospital or her job at all. Ironically, it was this problem that Jon thought he might be able to eliminate right away.

"Judy, have you toured the new senior independent-living center we opened last year? I know you don't want to put your parents in a nursing home and this could be the perfect alternative." He went on to describe the beautiful state-of-the-art facilities in detail. "And, it's only a few minutes away from the hospital."

"That sounds great." Judy seemed uncomfortable. "It's probably expensive."

"Hospital staff gets a generously reduced rate for family members. Let me make a quick call and I'll see if you can get in to see Charles Grant. Charles runs the show over there and he can answer any questions you might have. Let's see if he can meet with you today."

Jon wasn't sure, but Judy seemed to relax—like a weight had been lifted from her shoulders. Now, on to the other problems.

Jon wasn't aware that the program had created an increased workload for the accounting department. He didn't have a solution yet, but he had the next best thing right in front of him—the person closest to the problem.

"Judy, you've been with us a long time and I'd hate to lose you. I know that people relate well to you. Would you be willing to stay on and help me figure out how to fix the problems that you've listed here? Not just in the accounting department, but throughout the hospital?"

"Me?"

"I know it will require extra time on your part, so we'll bring in someone to help out with your routine work. I can't make you a counteroffer to what you'd be earning at your new job, but I can promise a salary review in six months. If we give you some peace of mind regarding your parents, and empower you to help your staff, would that give you incentive to stay?"

Judy smiled and agreed that it would. Jon handed her a copy of Cal's essay. "Here, I want you to read this. It'll give you an idea of how I'm tackling every problem you've revealed to me today and any we find out about in the future. When you're done, we'll start setting up some meetings with the department heads and charge nurses."

"Sounds good." As she stood up to go, Judy added, "You know, I really appreciate the time you've taken to talk to me this morning."

"I'm glad, Judy. I wish I had done it sooner."

SECTION 3

Fix It

Chapter 10

Reconnecting

I n less than one hour, Jon had managed to find out the real reasons behind Judy's resignation, and had enlisted a partner to help him illuminate other problems. *Illumination is about finding solutions that meet everyone's needs,* Jon mused, *not just the boss's, and it's not enough to just write it down.*

Eager to publicize his first success, Jon decided to send an e-mail to the retreat group:

From: Jon Saunders

To: West Coast Contingent

Re: Illumination

Just a note to let everyone know that I have taken the first steps in implementing Cal Deere's Illumination theory. If you remember, I had an important staff member submit her resignation. I had her come in and together we illuminated her problems. I believe she will be staying on, and I've asked her to assist me as we illuminate the entire hospital. Positive outcomes from negative thinking—who would have thought?

Within three days, everyone but Will had sent a reply congratulating Jon and reporting that they, too, were finding success with the Illuminate technique. On the fourth day, Jon was surprised to get a phone call from Cal himself.

"Cal, it is so good to hear from you! I've been worried. How are you doing?"

"Oh, much better, thanks. It was just a little scare. I'm going to have to put away my cherry tobacco and watch the diet and exercise a bit, but everything will be fine. How about you? I've been reading the e-mails. Seems you decided to go ahead and Illuminate, huh? Tell me what you've done."

Jon went on to explain Judy's situation in detail and told Cal that HR was hiring part-time help so Judy would be free to work with him. He also explained that HR was initially reluctant to admit that turnover could be related to employee satisfaction, pointing out that the exit interviews and surveys did not reflect a problem. After Jon reassured the department that he wasn't seeking blame, however, they agreed to review the questions on the form and survey. They discovered that their questions were so vague that employees weren't forced to reveal much about how they felt about their jobs. In addition, the questions didn't allow for negative feedback. A new, more specific exit interview was being crafted.

"Good, good." Cal said. "It seems like things are rolling right along."

"So far," said Jon.

"You know, I'll be in your area next week. Perhaps you could join me for supper on Wednesday. I'd love to meet your wife."

Jon rubbed his temples. "That would be terrific. Just let me know when you'll be here and I'll keep the date open. Cal, it was great to hear from you."

Jon got up to make copies of Cal's paper for all the department heads.

Chapter 11

Progress

J on was scheduled to meet with Donald, his boss, that day to recap the retreat. Jon also planned to introduce the Illuminate theory to explain how he was going to shore up the weak spots in the program and fix any preexisting problems.

Jon tried to prepare for the meeting. He read and reread Cal's paper, nearly committing it to memory. But Anne kept creeping into his thoughts. *Space or no space, she's my wife; it's time we talked this through.*

In the past, he and Anne had never run out of things to talk about. Today, however, when he picked up the phone, he didn't know what to say. His words came out stiff and rehearsed. "Hi, Anne. It's me. How are you?" *Jeez, I sound like a nervous teenager,* he thought.

"I'm good, Jon." Anne's voice sounded normal, making him feel more comfortable. "How are things at the hospital? Are you working out the problems there?"

Surprised that Anne had mentioned the hospital, Jon jumped on the chance to share what was going on. "Well, I got started on illuminating the negatives this week, and already I've found a few problems we weren't aware of. I even got Judy to retract her resignation. In fact, I've given her a bit of a promotion, and asked her to help steer the Illuminate concept at the hospital. So, I guess I'm feeling pretty good about the direction we're starting to move in now."

"I'm glad for you, Jon. I hope it works out."

Jon twirled a pencil between his fingers. "How about us, Anne? Are we going to work this out?"

It seemed like an eternity before a whisper of a sigh came through the phone. Anne replied, "I don't know, Jon. If we are, things are going to have to change."

"Okay, we can do that. Come home and we'll work it out. I'm sure we can—our marriage is better than most."

"You see?" Her voice started to sound pinched and high. "That's your way of looking at everything, Jon. You prefer to see only what's working and shove what isn't under the rug. We can't do that anymore. I don't want a good-enough marriage, I want a *great* marriage, and we can't have one if we don't stop hiding from our problems." She blew her nose too close to the phone. "I'm not ready to come home. There are still things I need to figure out for myself."

Jon closed his eyes in disappointment. "All right, Anne. But hurry. I miss you guys."

"I'll try. Good night." And then she hung up the phone.

Okay, so that could have gone better, Jon thought as he leaned back and stretched his arms behind his head to ease the tension in his shoulders. *But at least we're talking now. That's got to count for something.*

He picked up his notes and headed upstairs to Donald's office.

* * *

Jon's meeting with Donald didn't go quite as smoothly as he had hoped. He tried to talk about Illumination with the same passion as Cal had, and revealed the successes he had already witnessed as a result of his new approach. He talked about creating safe problem-solving cultures. He talked about the On a Mission program, and how much good it had done, and how much more good it could do once certain preexisting problems were illuminated.

As he had feared, though, Donald wasn't impressed. "Let me get this straight, Jon. Your plan to fix this hospital's problems is to get the staff to complain as much as possible?"

"Well, not quite . . ."

"That's exactly what it sounds like to me." Donald leaned forward on his desk. "You don't have any better strategy?"

111

Jon shook his head. "I'm telling you, this is the right strategy."

His boss heaved a sigh. "All right, then. Do what you want. But I'm watching you. If you can't turn this hospital around, I'll find someone who can."

When Jon left that night, he had been at the office 13 hours. Before leaving, though, he went to his office and sent an e-mail to his friends from the retreat:

From: Jon Saunders

To: West Coast Contingent

Re: Speed Bump

I told my boss how illuminating the negative is going to solve our problems at the hospital. He's letting me go forward with it, but he's expecting me to fail.
Wish me luck. I'm going to need it!

He turned off the computer and the lights, closed his door, and drove home to his empty house.

Chapter 12

On a Personal Note

J on stopped and picked up a sandwich and a salad on the way home. He pulled a cold beer out of the fridge and sat down on the couch with his dinner, a pad of paper, and a pen. Despite Donald's lack of enthusiasm, Jon was sure that illuminating the negative was the key to fixing the hospital's problems. Now, it was time to illuminate his marriage.

Step 1. Face it.
He'd faced it all right. Anne had made sure of that.
Step 2. Follow it.
He picked up the pen and wrote down what he knew:
PROBLEMS
Poor communication.
Hmmm. I've seen that one before.

He continued:

- Anne feels disrespected.
- Believes I don't know her anymore.
- My idea of a great marriage and her idea of a great marriage don't match.
- Resents the time I devote to the hospital.
- She feels alone.

115

On a Personal Note

Looking over the list, he contemplated each problem:

- Poor communication.

  I'll write her a letter telling her everything I feel. We used to write to each other a lot back in college. I'd take her letters out and read them over and over. She was a really good writer.

- Anne feels disrespected.

  I guess I've been judging the value of our work based on who gets paid the most. If her work is that important to her, it needs to be that important to me. I'll have to work on this one.

- Believes I don't know her.

  Of course I know her. But if she wants me to know how she feels or what she's thinking, she's going to have to speak up. We'll have to work on creating an environment in which she's comfortable expressing herself.

- The good-enough marriage.

  That's it. That's the big problem. And the first step to fixing it is improving communication, so that's where I'm going to start.

Leaving the rest of the list for later, Jon spent the next two hours writing a letter to Anne. He stopped and started over several times. By the time he finished, it was late. He closed his eyes. The last thing he saw was the list of problems he had written when he sat down. It was in the center of the coffee table, face up.

* * *

Jon woke up at 5 A.M. with a stiff neck from sleeping on the couch. He showered, dressed, and went into the living room, picking up his letter to Anne. He poured a cup of coffee and sat down to read what he hoped would open a dialogue between the two of them.

It was a good letter, causing him to smile as he remembered things they had done together— plans they had made, welcoming Ben into their lives, applauding each other's success.

Jon bit his lip. Anne had applauded his success. Maybe he hadn't thought to cheer her on because she had willingly chosen to step away from her high-powered career. Now he realized that she needed to know he was still proud of her.

He picked up his pen and added this last paragraph to the letter:

Anne, I have been illuminated. You are a great wife and mother, but you are also much more. I am committed to our marriage, and

117

On a Personal Note

I am willing to do anything I can to show you that I love and support you. Your happiness is everything to me. Together we can create a marriage that is great in both of our eyes. Think about it.

Love,

Jon

Chapter 13

Positive Effects

When Jon logged into his computer the following morning, there were several e-mails from the West Coast group. Every one of them encouraged him to keep illuminating the negative, despite his boss's lack of support. Illumination was working for them.

Vahe had been concerned that his research facility was lagging behind the competition, who seemed to launch award-winning innovations almost every year. After illuminating the negative with his research teams, he was dismayed to learn that his scientists didn't feel they had time to develop new creative concepts that might fail, so they were spending their days refining and improving the ones they already knew would succeed. They needed some incentive to work harder and break out of the box. Vahe decided to implement a reward program. For every award won or every successful licensing deal, the creative team responsible for the technology or product would win a cash prize and additional vacation time.

Illumination had given Lois a terrific way to figure out how to increase brand awareness and revenue for her chain of jewelry stores. By illuminating the negative, she found out that salespeople refused to mention the company's web site for fear of losing in-store sales and commissions. Now, every new piece of jewelry is first launched on the web site, which then directs customers to the web site if they wished to order. After placing their order, customers can wait to receive their jewelry in a week or so in the mail, or they could get it immediately by declaring which retail store they would use to pick up their order. There, they would find it ready and waiting. Lois discovered that almost 40 percent of customers made additional purchases when they came to the store to pick up their online order. It was now in the salespeople's best interest to urge customers to check the web site frequently so they could be first in line for the latest look. "I never would have known that my salespeople resented the Facebook page and web site if I hadn't illuminated the negative. Now I've got three ways for customers to engage with my brand, and they're all working together!"

Reading these testimonials renewed Jon's confidence that he was on the right track. He looked up from his computer and was surprised to find the nurse manager standing in his doorway. Millie did not look happy.

"Just what is this about?" She thrust a copy of Cal's essay toward him.

Looks like Judy had that distributed to the staff right away. She's on top of things, Jon thought.

Millie was protective of her nurses. She was very good at her job and Jon valued her input tremendously. "Sit down, Millie. Let's talk. What's on your mind?"

"This Illuminate the Negative concept, that's what. We've spent all this time restructuring everything so that our patients would have a better experience. And I believe they do. But now it looks like you're ready to implement another shakeup. Make up your mind, Jon. I can't keep asking my nurses to jump through hoops because administration can't decide what they want to do."

"I understand. I promise you, illuminating the negative is going to make things easier, not harder. It's not going to require any additional work from your nurses."

"It had better not. We're at the end of our rope as it is," Millie grumbled.

Jon was surprised by her attitude. "I thought you supported the On a Mission program?"

"I did . . . I do," said Millie, her face softening. "Look, for the first time, my nurses feel empowered to use their judgment and devote more attention to their patients. At last they don't feel taken for granted."

"I don't understand, then," Jon said. "What's the problem?"

"The problem is that every one of us is on the verge of burnout. I'm not talking about fatigue,

Positive Effects

which we all suffer from. I mean the kind of stress and overwork that causes us to make mistakes. I should know," Millie looked into her lap, "I almost killed a woman last week."

Jon let this sink in. He asked softly, "What happened?"

When Millie looked up, she was on the brink of tears. "I can't really say. It was at the end of my third shift—one of my nurses left to get her MD so we're shorthanded right now. Anyway, I brought Mrs. Jacobson her meds. I handed her the cup of water and I was about to give her the pills when I realized that they were the wrong ones. I had switched hers with those of Mrs. Ruby down the hall. Thank the Good Lord I noticed. Either one of these patients could have died if they'd taken each other's meds. I could have set us up for another malpractice suit, and this one we would have deserved to lose."

Jon was silent for a minute and said, "Well, your patients didn't die, and there was no cause for a suit. You caught the mistake and it won't happen again."

Millie wiped her eyes. "Jon, I love taking care of people. My nurses do, too. We are team players, committed to this hospital and our patients. You'll never hear us whine. But if something isn't done to relieve our stress, no, I cannot promise that something like that won't happen again. Burnout is a serious problem, and it's not going to go away just because we keep repeating 'I think I can, I think can.'"

"I hear you," said Jon. "See, that's what Illuminate is all about. You've just shed light on a problem I didn't know existed. What can I do to ease the nurses' stress?"

"I have no idea. I haven't taken the time to think about it, either."

"I wish I'd known about this problem sooner."

"I thought it was pointless to bring it up when I had no solution to offer."

Jon said, "That's my fault, Millie. But I've recently learned that sometimes just holding a light up to the problem is a valid first step toward solving it. Now that we know the problem exists, we can get everyone involved in fixing it. Have you asked your nurses for their ideas?"

"No, I didn't want to open up a can of worms."

"Well, let's go ahead and open it up. Provident's nurses are the best out there and I value their opinions."

"All right, let me talk to a few of them and see if I can get some insight." For the first time since she'd appeared in Jon's office, Millie smiled. "Imagine, being asked to complain! I'll let you know what comes of it."

Jon felt good after Millie left. So far, illuminating the negative was having a very positive effect on his world.

Chapter 14

Hope

A few days later, when Jon got home, he flipped through the mail and found exactly what he was looking for—a letter from Anne. The familiar handwriting jumped out at him, and he opened the envelope as quickly as he could without tearing its contents.

Dear Jon,

Your letter made me smile, even laugh. The memories are wonderful, and it was nice to be reminded of them again.

This time apart has been good for me, although I know it has been stressful for you. When I left I was angry, but I realize now that the problems in our marriage have not been entirely your fault. Thank you for being patient with me and for giving me the time I needed to decide what I really want—and I do want very much to be close to you again.

This marriage deserves another chance. I believe if we can continue to work on it as we are now, we'll have more than a great marriage; we'll have an illuminated one.

Love,

Anne

Jon was excited. There was hope! He quickly grabbed the phone and called his wife. His words rushed together as he asked her to go to dinner. They agreed on the following night. Jon would have loved to talk, but Anne didn't give him a chance, ending the conversation with "I'll see you then."

Chapter 15

Sweet Successes

The next morning, Millie knocked on his office door and stuck her head in.

"Oh, good, you're here," she exclaimed. "I've got some news for you. I had a good talk with my staff yesterday. They were relieved to know they were being heard. Frankly, they're all exhausted. I don't think they can continue at this rate much longer."

"Did you find out what's causing the additional stress?" Jon asked.

"Well, there are several factors, but one grabbed my attention right away because it seems to me it's something we might be able to fix right away. The nurses' break room is just not conducive to taking a break!"

"How's that?"

"First, it's right next door to the nurses' station. They're constantly interrupted when they're on a break, which means there is no opportunity to relax at all. Second, it looks and smells like a closet that hasn't been opened since the seventies. We're supposed to use it for stress-relief, but honestly, I can't spend more than five minutes in it before my blood pressure goes up."

Jon got up and asked Millie to walk with him to the break room. It was a depressing place. Orange and green plastic chairs lined walls that hadn't seen a fresh coat of paint in years. A small TV was perched on a milk crate. An old poster advised the proper way to lift to avoid injury.

"I see what you mean, Millie. This place could certainly use some updating. I'm thinking curtains and fresh paint, new upholstered furniture— maybe even a recliner or two. We can afford to make some cosmetic changes, but the truth is we need to look at another location, because this certainly isn't big enough. The problem is we don't have the funds for a relocation or a renovation."

"We need to find them," Millie argued. "Nursing is a stressful job with a lot of responsibility. It's difficult and maybe impossible to continue that level of stress for ten or twelve hours without a chance to relax."

"I agree. Let me see what I can do. What else did the nurses suggest?" Jon asked.

"They want more say in scheduling. I was thinking, what if we created a council that would allow them to express their concerns regarding scheduling, policy, and procedures that affect their work environment? That way they'd be sure their voices were heard."

"You think that would help ease the burnout rate?"

"I really do," Millie said.

"Then let's make it happen."

Before Jon knew it, it was time to call it a day. Today he would be sure to leave his office on time—he was having dinner with his wife. Before he left, however, he sent an elated e-mail to his friends from the retreat to tell them how illuminating the negative was allowing him to eliminate more and more problems from his life.

Chapter 16

Finding Answers

Jon stopped on the way home and picked up his dry cleaning. He spent a few extra minutes showering and shaving for his date with Anne. Then, he made sure he got out the door in time to pick her up.

Ben answered the door and was a little disappointed that he wasn't invited to come along, but Jon explained that he would pick him up Saturday; tonight was "Mommy and Daddy time." Anne appeared behind Ben and Jon felt like it had been months since he'd seen her. He almost felt like he was on a first date, a little nervous to be alone with her.

They walked out of the house. Jon leaned over and gave Anne a kiss on the cheek. "You look lovely, Anne."

"Thank you. It's been a long time since you've told me that." Jon realized that she was right. Small talk took up most of the ride to the little French restaurant, which was known for its intimate atmosphere and extensive wine list. Jon pulled a chair out for Anne and sat down, wondering where to start.

Anne was the first to speak. "I started keeping a journal again. It helped me make some sense of my feelings."

"You used to do that years ago. Why did you quit?" Jon replied.

"It didn't seem important anymore. I had you and Ben. I had my work. But now I'm finding I'm enjoying it—very much, actually. When I sit down to write, I feel inspired. I'm thinking of applying for a job at *ArtSeen*."

"You want to write for a magazine? A full-time job?"

"Not exactly. I'd like to be home when Ben gets home from school. Now that the project at the children's hospital is done, I thought I could set up a small office at home and write on a part-time basis."

"That's a great idea. You know, I'm going to be delegating more work and I've got some good people on my side at the hospital. I think I can arrange for a more flexible schedule so I can be home to help you more often. How about it?"

"I really appreciate that."

Jon leaned in. "You'll see, Anne. We're going to illuminate every problem we have. And we're going to illuminate every problem we face in the future. It's going to be different. It's going to be better."

Anne smiled and speared a carrot glistening with butter.

"There you go with illuminating the negative again."

"I'm telling you, it's the most powerful and empowering concept I've come across in a long time." Jon twirled his food around his fork. "Speaking of illuminating the negative, Cal is coming to town on Wednesday and we're meeting for dinner. I'd really like it if you would join us."

"I think I'd enjoy that, too, Jon. It's a date."

Hours later, after lingering over dessert long enough to earn their waitress a fat tip for not pushing them out of their seats, Jon dropped Anne off at her mother's door. This time she was the one who leaned forward to give him a kiss on the cheek. "Good night, Jon. I'll see you soon."

On the ride home, Jon was no longer sad or lonely. He was excited about the plans he was making with his wife.

Chapter 17

Surprise

The West Coast group who had met at the retreat had all shared the news of the success they'd experienced by illuminating the negative. The only person no one had heard from was Will Franklin, which was exactly why Jon was astounded to read an e-mail from him at the beginning of the next week:

To: Jon Saunders

From: Will Franklin

Re: Nurses' Break Room

Dear Jon,

I have been reading with interest, and I admit some skepticism, about everyone's positive experience with illuminating the negative. While I would like to see hard data supporting its efficacy, I cannot help but be impressed with the success you've enjoyed.

In addition, I confess that since we parted I have continued to replay our discussion about company values. Perhaps I've immersed myself too long in a world defined by the value of numbers, and have forgotten to place enough value on values themselves. I admire your determination to uphold the values espoused by your hospital and all the hardworking people who do their best every day to bring comfort and support to those who need them. Though normally it is our goal at Dobbins to invest in moneymaking ventures, we have decided that it is time to invest in some hardworking human capital for a change.

I am pleased to inform you that we would like to contribute $80,000 toward a new break room for your nurses. It is our hope and expectation that they will receive a state-of-the-art retreat, complete with wall-mounted flat-panel television, Harmonic Healthcare Music System, and headphones. We would also like to offer them a massaging recliner, microwave, and refrigerator for their convenience.

In addition, we'd like to urge the hospital to apply for Magnum status. As you know, Magnum-designated hospitals are widely known to provide the highest nursing standards in the country. Magnum status has been proven to improve patient confidence, increase salaries, lower turnover, and increase overall revenue. With Magnum status, your nurses will be publicly recognized as the best in their field.

The application fees for Magnum status are steep, and the process will likely require some of your nurses to further their education. To that end, Dobbins Venture Capital will sponsor the department, covering all application fees, tuition costs, and any other funds necessary up to $300,000 for the nurses to achieve their goal.

I hope that you will allow us to work with you to bring your nurses and other hospital staff the security and public recognition they deserve. I will be officially contacting Donald with our offer and suggestions forthwith.

Sincerely,

Will Franklin

Jon's mouth dropped open. He reread the e-mail again. *Wow!* He jumped up and immediately reached out for the phone to call Donald, then changed his mind and decided to call Millie. *So that's why Donald wanted me to get to know Will during the retreat. He knew they were looking for a new charitable project. Well, I'll be,* Jon thought.

* * *

A few days later, Jon watched his wife and Cal talk over cocktails. They almost seemed to have forgotten he was at the table. Jon was pleased to see the two of them getting along so wonderfully.

Their conversation was interrupted when the waiter came to take their order. Jon seized the opportunity to tell them both about Will Franklin's donation to the nurses' break room and his group's sponsorship.

Cal congratulated him with a firm slap on the back. Anne leaned over to give him a small hug. They discussed the hospital, Anne's new career plans, and Cal's business. Cal was contemplating semiretirement in the upcoming year. His health scare had made him realize he wanted to spend more time with his family in his senior years. "Work to live, not live to work, right, Jon?" Cal winked.

"Right," Jon said. He reached under the table to lightly squeeze his wife's hand. She squeezed back.

The group parted ways in the parking lot, promising to stay in touch. Jon drove Anne home, but didn't drive her to her mother's. He pulled up to their own driveway. There was something he wanted to show her.

Over the weekend, Jon had purchased a computer system and added a new printer complete with fax machine and scanner. He took her into the guest room, where he had set everything up on an old desk.

"I didn't get you a desk, Anne. I thought you should pick out exactly what you wanted. And an office chair, too. I want you to make this your own space."

Her eyes glassy with tears, Anne reached out to hug him, speechless. But Jon wasn't. "Welcome home, Anne."

Epilogue

A year brought a world of change to Jon Saunders.

Anne and Ben moved back home, and although Jon and his wife still encountered occasional problems, like most married people do, they learned to deal with them head-on. Eventually, there was almost no need for illumination in their relationship, for they kept their problems in the light, where they could be seen and dealt with.

Cal did indeed retire from his old job, but within months was deeply involved in a new consulting firm he'd formed with a small group of his most trusted friends and colleagues. He called the new firm Beacon.

One day, Cal and his wife joined Jon and Anne for dinner in their new home.

"What a cozy house," Cal commented,

Anne smiled. "We like it. It's smaller than the old one, but even though the family is growing," she put her hand on her swollen belly, "we wanted a home that reinforced a sense of togetherness. We also didn't want to be weighed down by all that stuff we'd acquired over the years. We've kept the antiques we both love, but otherwise we want to keep our lives simple and, quite frankly, easy to clean!"

Cal's wife, a matronly, kind-eyed woman, nodded. "You'll never regret it."

"Jon, how did your ribbon-cutting ceremony go last week?" Cal asked, sipping a glass of red wine. "Was the nurses' break room a hit?"

"It sure was. Will was there, and we gave him the honor of cutting the ribbon. We also introduced him to the nurses who are training to bring the hospital to Magnum status. I think even Will was surprised at how much the nurses appreciate the challenge and how they are looking forward to the recognition that Magnum status brings. And now that we've solved the underlying problems that were holding it back, the On a Mission program has finally been able to work the way it's supposed to. Turnover is almost zero percent, revenue is up, and the hospital is thriving and getting a lot of positive attention. I actually got an apology from Donald for doubting my methods. I'm glad I stayed long enough see the whole process through to the end."

"And now I'm looking forward to having you join me at the Beacon family. By the way, when exactly is your newest member going to make an appearance?" Cal asked.

Jon smiled and reached over to touch his wife's stomach. "We have two months before the big day," he said glancing at Anne. She had never been more beautiful. He hoped the baby was a little girl who would look just like her mother.

"I'll have just enough time to finish my latest article," Anne said. "And my editor says she'll be looking forward to hearing more story ideas when I'm ready to start working again after the baby is born."

Suddenly, Ben came blazing into the room. He had just returned from baseball practice. "Dad, can you practice with me? I'm the starting pitcher Friday!"

"I'll throw a few with you, Ben. If you don't mind playing with an old man, that is," Cal said with a twinkle in his eye.

"Well, okay, but you think you can handle my fastball?" Ben asked.

Jon interrupted, "Your fastball? Don't you need to practice your curve ball? You've got to work on those changeups."

"*Nah.* Curve balls are hard. I'm just gonna throw my fastball. I'm always good at that."

Jon looked at his son and said, "Wait a minute, you're just going to ignore your curve ball?"

"Coach Danson said my fast pitch is really good. Why should I mess with a curve ball?"

Jon looked up and caught Anne's eye over Ben's head. Before either had a chance to speak, their friend interjected.

Stooping down, Cal said to their son, "Ben, what do you know about mushrooms?"

Their son was about to be illuminated.

Acknowledgments

As always, there seem to be too many people to thank for contributing to this project. My writing, consulting, and speaking businesses are inspired by my observations of and interactions with a fantastic group of clients, employees, colleagues, friends, and of course, my amazing family.

To my dear family and circle of friends, I am deeply grateful for your presence in my life and the influence you have had on my thoughts and my heart.

Special thanks to the wonderful people at Aesthetic Audio Systems, The Performance Technology Group, Dr. Adriane Levy Corbin, David Gilman, Phillip Wexler, Donna DeGutis, Harry Paul, Mitch Axelrod, Greg S. Reid, and Melanie Riveira.

Thanks as well to Anne Wayman for kickstarting this manuscript, Cordelia Brown for her impressive writing and creativity, Patti McKenna for enhancing the characters and story, Doug Beck and Robert S. Levy for keeping it accurate and orderly, and Stephanie Land, editor par excellence, for her contribution of "illuminating" the manuscript.

To Jenna Leah Corbin and Benjamin Ari Corbin, thanks for illuminating every aspect of my life.

And to my wonderful publishing team—beginning with my literary agent, Bill Gladstone of Waterside Productions, and the great team at John Wiley & Sons Inc., headed up by Shannon Vargo with Beth Zipko and Kate Lindsay—I am very grateful for your keen expertise and guidance.

For further information or to schedule a speaking engagement or Illuminate Training by David Corbin contact:

David Corbin's Performance Technology Group
858-748-6060
E-mail: melanie@davidcorbin.com
Web site: www.davidcorbin.com